Poems for Cosmic Lovers

Jeffrey Gale F.R.S.A.

AuthorHouse™ UK
1663 Liberty Drive
Bloomington, IN 47403 USA
www.authorhouse.co.uk
Phone: 0800.197.4150

Published by AuthorHouse 08/31/2019

ISBN: 978-1-7283-8404-7 (sc)
ISBN: 978-1-7283-8403-0 (e)

authorHOUSE®

Contents

Mt. Kailash - West Flank.

Front Cover: East flank of Mt. Kailash, in Himalayas, India (part annexed by China).

This domed summit mountain is the most sacred for both Hindus and Buddhists. It makes a very special Pilgrimage for them to walk around it, said to be the abode of Lord Shiva, god of powerful transmutation and reincarnation. The South face of Kailash is reflected in the Lake of the Sun, Manasarova. This painting is part of a series of different views of Kailash.

4

Poems for Cosmic Lovers

2016 - 2018

This is the first collection of poems by Jeffrey Gale. They range in subject from cosmic pastoral to cosmic space.

The aim is to cover themes of human interest, which are eternal. The dilemmas of human existence and beauties of wildlife in landscapes inspire the author.

Others describe aspects of our lovely Earth as metaphors for life now, in my searching, questioning consciousness. I have travelled this world far and wide making meditational paintings in inspiring places, especially India Himalayas: - See book covers and illustrations inside.

He has lived in Devon for about 25 years and regards it as his spiritual home. Most of that period was spent in Totnes, so the River Dart and Dartmoor figure in some poems.

"The good Earth speaks through my Art, whether painting or poetry, and true Art must always be a mystery" (September, 2018).

Most were composed specially for our "Poetry and Music" program, held monthly and broadcast on Sound Art Radio studios in Dartington, Totnes, Devon (102.5 FM).

Your feedback appreciation is welcome.

Contact me on tel. 01803 866349 (pref); or jeffrey@worldpeacegardensnet.org

Jeffrey G. Pubs.ltd

Birth of a Planet

Where would we be without the sun,
Deep as the pit and nowhere to run. ?

* * *

Where would we be without air to breathe,
sharing Earths destiny in making the weave.

* * *

Where would we be without the rain,
to nourish the dust into soil again.

* * *

Where would we be without the trees,
Delighting, shading and bonding good earth with ease.

* * *

Where would we be without the fire,
to stoke our souls with burning desire.

* * *

Where would we be without the sea,
the untamed beast just longing to be free!

* * *

Where would we be without your love,
to make this Earth like Heaven above.

* * *

How lucky we are to be born on this planet,
especially if its England,
the self-styled birth Queen of Europe remains,
Where all words are free, but not all people,
And politics is double – talk, or simply profane.

* * *

The Nature of Reality and Peace

Where, oh where shall we find peace within this
world?
Perhaps the simple answer lies beyond our minds,
For our frenetic thoughts have yet to find
the peace we clearly crave,
Instead they fight within themselves to find some
resolution!

*   *   *

What's the use, you say, when human brain's designed
to keep our senses sensitive,
transforming thoughts to actions,
While beyond all this they have idea,
and these create our arty, sciences, music or poetry,
but sadly too, conflicting ideologies, religions, politics
do rage!

*   *   *

Beyond this mindful mess must come, some deeply
bedded harmony,
like light and life itself,
whose waves do emanate to permeate our beings,
with many a welcome warm caress!

*   *   *

How can we hope for peace,
when light itself is radiant from fire,
the sun we love so much is but a raging cauldron,
While Seas of our dear Earth do gulp the Sun,
to spew it back in sheets of rain!

*   *   *

The splendours of our natural world could die,

and our poor brains and body too, become a shrivelled
husk,
without its daily blessing we call rain,
carrier of Consciousness, memory of other worlds,
the ultimate connector of connectedness.

*   *   *

Consider now the Nature of Reality …
Beyond what we call substance lies one vastly space,
within whose empty confines there is mystery,
And there can someone surely find the answer to our
quest for peace,
for Consciousness pervades this emptiness,
Not travelling, but simply Being!

*   *   *

Dart my Heart

Dart my heart, you are the embodiment of continuous life …
Slowly this bright craft carries me down towards the open sea,
While I breathe the Herringull's tangy air,
this River breathes the waxing Moons embrace.
Very slowly this mystic stream has lulled my consciousness,
till thus seduced, I'm once more one with all the World.

*   *   *

Floating in a dream of greens, these ten thousand Oaks
drift by, like passive guardians to my voyage,
while I move slowly down to drown within the ultimate Sea,
from whence I risen in the Angelic clouds to fall again as rain
sweeping over Dartmoor heights.

*   *   *

This Dart is the very heart beat of our Totnes Town;
Lucky I've been to live by the Weir for many years,
able to see the daily rise and fall of tides,
Otters diving, flashing King fishers and stately gliding Swans,
While the lonely Heron stands with glinting eye,
ready to snatch a passing fish.

*   *   *

Sometimes a fierce storm over Dartmoor
would make the Weir become a roaring cauldron boiling cataract,
Here is the grand change point, the outpouring of our greatest life-giver, the ever throbbing fuser of our land to sea. Our ancestors felt her power, her life-long energy …
Over the wide world they settled by springs, streams or river,
needing her daily sustenance and blessings.

*   *   *

Our delicate skin needs and longs for her touch,
when we bathe in her water we Baptise ourselves, and feel renewed.
Water, the greatest mystery of this Planet has unlimited capacity to cleanse and renew.

*   *   *

In many special ways our ancestors worshipped the Goddess of Water.
From source to sea this River winds around her latent Staff of Hermes. The Dart herself weaves her sensual erotic curves about this unseen pole, a straight line from Outer Froward Point (near Kingswear) to Brownstone Tower, to Lower Noss Point, to Fire Beacon Hill (Dittisham), to White Rock, to Sharpham House, to Longmarsh Park to St Marys Church and Swallowfields, Totnes; Staverton Bridge, Buckfastleigh old Church and Weir, Hembury Castle, Holme Woods Dart and Bench Tor.
This ley line continues with its outstanding markers all the way to Dartmeet, where Dart divides to find her sources high on Dartmoor.

The Hawk

Slow in the watchful sky, this Hawk rotates,
Mindful in the gleaming eye of a vole,
how I envy that so careless windblown freedom,
within the slightest tilt of wing or feather,
he gathers the air to his mind, always ready.

*   *   *

His giddy range can see the greenly detailed land;
Let me enter that mind to feel the air's embrace,
always stroking his body in myriad fine-tuned senses,
he's bathed and cleaned within the gate that we may fear!

*   *   *

Look how this stern eye holds freedom,
captures the world in awe without concern,
except perhaps for a fearful prey,
whose tiny life is swiftly snatched away!

*   *   *

Oh hanging Hawk, can you be the guardian of Gods secrets,
Can you know the freedom of Being
we earthbound creatures crave?
Just let me enter your mindful mind this while,
to sense the nature of my body is less than air,
whose spiritual essence can also join you in your flight.

*   *   *

Where, I wonder do you alight at night?
Must there be some rocky cleft high upon a windy cliff,
or spare upon a branch of that majestic Redwood.
While there do you dream of juicy voles,
or fierce fights with a pitching jealous rival?

*   *   *

Passion

How can one live without passion?
The best can be sublime, like the heated love affair,
the worst murderous!

*   *   *

Passion for me is not suffering, but a driver;
sometimes even an inspiration …
Some of my best poems come from a kind of
frustration;
so often not realised the way I'd like,
or not built at all!

*   *   *

Making paintings and poems is a wonderful outlet
for me;
without this creative work I would quickly atrophy.
For me creativity and passion are often linked;
strong feelings generate passion, and they can interact
wonderfully.

*   *   *

Blessed is the being with passion,
tho' dangerous without creative outlets.
As a driver of dedication it is sublime,
As a driver of violence or self-destruction, it ends in
tragedy.

*   *   *

Those who know passion know life.
To live fully is to live passionately.
True Christians have a passionate identity with Christ,
Buddhists aim to avoid suffering by acts of random
kindness,
meditation and non-violent living.

*   *   *

For me passionate music and poetry are the most
moving …
Hardly a baby is born without passion!
A great painting or any expressive work of art comes
thru' the magic of passion.
We humans are born out of passion, and we hold it in
our hearts
for all our lives – long live Passion!

*   *   *

The Space Between

If you insist on asking who am I?
The reply I'd give is, "just listen to your breathing …
and relax into the tiny space where outbreath ends,
for this is where you come to find the light
of who you truly are, within this moment out of time.

* * *

Your mind will quickly interrupt saying :-
"I am who you are, a great collection of memories,
experiences, thoughts, ideas, ambitions, sorrows and relationships,
this tiny space between you say is you,
is just no more than that, just space!"

* * *

Imagine your breathing is like great sea waves
where your outward breath has reached the foaming crest,
And then this hidden portal opens just for you,
to plunge into the wider realms of heightened consciousness.

* * *

It's strange you say, that when I fall into that space,
the problems of the day just seem to go away;
Instead this warmly buoyant overwhelming peace immerses me,
and I find my true self inside a golden garden paradise of delights.

* * *

Here inside this portal of peace,
lies freedom from agitations of my mind,
and here must surely be my true identity,
my loving God of spirit within.

* * *

Grey Winter Meditation

Come, come you Sun,
to break this dull grey mantle heavy heavens,
Please pierce the wool with your welcome sword,
so my cold body can feel your warmth,
and walk away outside my mind.

*   *   *

Come, come you Sun,
to fill my heart and mind with joy,
and cast beyond dull weighty thoughts,
to fire my tardy mind with brilliant visions,
way outside the woolly sea above.

*   *   *

Come, come you slothful Sun,
slash through this cloying cloak,
to where the air is clear,
and Sun can see no barriers,
where swallows fly so high to test their freedom.

*   *   *

Come, come you warming Sun,
these days grow small,
and shorten time to write this glowing verse,
too brief to ponder life in all its timeless splendours.

*   *   *

Come, come you giving Sun,
Must I await your golden gifts,
while Earth down here rotates so fast,
I must so sadly miss some tiny cracks of light,
that give me hope these colder shortening days.

*   *   *

Life, Light and Love

Dear life, how long must I remain a Bramacharya?
Your beauty holds my heart,
so take my hand and hold it to your waist,
that I may now begin to taste your shape and scented
forms,
that have too long denied my primal birth's desire
to satisfy my rising, avid longing thirst …
First food, then gorgeous touch and glimpse of form
beyond.

*   *   *

This memory of baby me
remains so deeply lodges in heart and mind,
why should it ever find another place
to hide away, behind my prayers for purity;
Although my will is strong, in time it must so surely
make
its presence felt, until fulfilled.

*   *   *

Dear heart, I bow before your mindful dreams,
that long to find themselves in mystic arts,
not just to make another child,
instead to make fine paintings in transcendent beauty,
the kind of scenes that gather other souls like flowers,
then casts them all around the world
till they may one day land, to sprout again
in others minds to fire creations and ideas.

*   *   *

This human world of ours in turnings thrives in our
connexions,

And so we're floating on these minds of light-filled
consciousness,
carried on our magic carpet that gives an overview of
lives unfolding.
Fly thus, or move in darkness, half aware of who or
what we are.

*   *   *

Let's board this golden ship of faith in Life.
Enjoying the warm celestial winds,
like birds of Paradise, we too can fly.

*   *   *

Spring Storm, in Lyme-Regis

Now one feels the wild wind – like beast
that's longing to escape,
hurling itself against this shuttered house
with such ferocity, I fear to breach my door …

*　　*　　*

Still, this is life, a need to step outside
my cosy boundaries into this fearful fray,
though the gale slaps my face,
she whips my cap away,
this cold stimulation starts a rigor in my mind
that too much sloth has dulled.

*　　*　　*

Bent low to cut the storm
she tears my clothes and draws my cloak
high into the roaring air, swirling and flying up,
just loving a new-found freedom.

*　　*　　*

Mindfully, I wonder how the sea can be in such a storm,
so turning, let this wind thrust me down the hill
to see the spray pounding up up the cliffs in demented fury!
While breathless, my mind responds profoundly
to this glorious gale, and if the stream allows,
I'll fight my weaving way back home,
to flop down by the fire, and write a poem.

*　　*　　*

Earth's mantle has ways of snatching you up
to shake you like a rag-doll,
sometimes a blessing, sometimes a disaster, always a thrill;
the unpredictability of life is what I love, you too?

*　　*　　*

Birth

From the gleam within your eyes,
And the mutual marrying consciousness,
Has brought this being into life;
And this Being, so endowed, has made
the choice with aid of some rare alchemy
to be a boy or girl beginning …

*   *   *

What miracle is this you need to say
Can make the loving gleam into a soul
who wants to build an embryo
from seeds, so random cast in sensual passion.

*   *   *

So here within the warming womb,
the embryonic mind has will to make a babe,
with food the mother must provide for this
this other human slowly, slowly grows.

*   *   *

In turn the mother knows a lovely feeling of wellbeing,
And thanks the gift of life for this,
With blessings given free all around by friends,
who wish to celebrate this magical event.

*   *   *

Now months have passed, the babe makes energetic signs
it wishes to escape the warming waters of the womb
to enter light, with painful push and shove …
Oh my! the woman screams, as midwife tries to soothe,
the tiny head appears, then body with lung's
first breath drawn in, and outward in a cry! …
Our mother holds it to her breast,
with grateful tears of thankfulness and joy.

*   *   *

Water, Earth and Sun

How strangely beautiful this miraculous marriage
of Water, Earth and Sun …
For this brings all Life, all Love, all sustenance,
to all the teeming, living fabric of this fair Planet.

*   *   *

Can we humanity embrace the goodly Earth,
as we would a lover or a Muse?
For this Planet needs to breathe as we do,
And the fertile skin needs the natural nutrients
to complete the Sacred Circle.

*   *   *

These natural flows must not be lost,
else all the Beings just wondering this sphere
may one day return to find a desert …
What future for our children or our trees,
If we neglect to help in some small way,
to join the Sacred Circle.

*   *   *

Can we wrap this girdle round our waists, lest we
forget?
Like our lungs she needs to breathe and sigh
below the endless fiery Sun, for then,
there is water, there is air there is abundant greens.
Our people now do have the choice to hold this
delicate balance aloft,
or lose it in the pressing waves of mindless
materialism.

*   *   *

Walking by the shore, we can watch the wind-blown
sea breathing,
feel, see and hear the ocean's steady beat;
Here is the chance to let our minds be one with this,
while slowing down, and letting passing thoughts
dissolve,
can we become the spirit of the sea,
And so enjoin the universal consciousness,
to find our deeper selves rejoicing, this must be me!

*   *   *

The eternal symphony of the sea
Can show us how to be more peaceful, to lose our
minds,
enjoining in the meditation.

*   *   *

"Venice after Turner"

**<u>Venetian Islands,</u> recomposed vistas of San Giorgio Maggiore, Zattere and Lido. *For me Venice is the most civilised and beautiful of all European Cities. This painting was made after my first visit there on my way to India in 1970, when I stayed with Daniello, who made large sound sculptures (installations) on Lido Island. Recently I was a delegate in the Festival for the Earth, themed on global warming and climate change. This gave me splendid opportunities to enjoy many exotic Renaissance interiors of this great city of Venice. This time I stayed with Roberto, a surrealist painter, and his wife, who showed me his studio in an old Fort near Mestre.*

Cosmic Freedom

Where there's water there is Life …
When Life began on Earth our fireball Sun
did ask:- " How did you dear life begin?"
Was it for sure when you my sister Water
reached out to greet me Sun,
to make a magic blend in Earth and Sea,
when plankton turned from brown to green.

*   *   *

Let pass a million millennia the first green shoots
appear,
Any tiny flowers do later grace the golden deserts
with colours …
Yet much later still the minute flies appeared,
to reach inside to fertilise these miniature blooms
How then the most miraculous of all,
when insects seem to sprout new wings,
and butterflies are seen, air born in many gorgeous
shades.

*   *   *

Who commanded them the ocean's fish to fly?
If you have fins and tails to leap above the waves,
given a million years or so, can stretch those fins,
to find the semblance of wings, these hybrid fish birds
come gliding slowly down, to dive at tasty butterflies,
them safely landing in the lush green canopy …

*   *   *

And so the heavy blundering dinosaurs,
must remain strangers to this air born world,
stuck in gravitational mud, jealous of these new bird
freedoms,
growling with a shake of a muddy claw into the sky.

*   *   *

Given a few more trillion years, the dynamic man
appears,
dreaming high on a mountain perch, and thinking …
"Oh I wish I could fly!"
One day for sure with feather light wings on alloy
bones,
I will glide off this rock to catch convection lifts,
to soar, then slowly fall, amazed to view the
rolling tapestry of fields and forests below.

*   *   *

Dart Voyage

Drawn by the swelling tide,
We board the mythic yacht,
to navigate the ancient artery named Dart,
towards the distant sea.

*   *   *

Like a silver swan, the craft glides forth
above a shimmering River,
and we feel her cutting a surging furrow,
fast pulling our ship past the curling mighty Oaks,
we feel at one with her irresistibly conscious mind,
like a force in the air beyond the wind,
beyond Aeolian gods, beyond the swelling
Spinnaker …

*   *   *

Here we are, on a flying magic carpet,
feeling a special kind of aerial elation,
flying out of time into the minds of earliest sailors,
who dreamed of gold and luscious fruits in distant
lands.

*   *   *

The dream we have of breaking out the confines of
this Isle,
into the glittering sea of colourful fantasies.
This ancient pull is always there
within the construct of our minds and soul,
our longing is to breathe the salt-sea air,
And hear the pounding rhythm of the crashing waves.

*   *   *

Yet once out there we may discern our distant land,
With yet another kind of longing,

That of the fire and friendly earth beneath our feet;
so once our voyage is over,
we then can celebrate our homes, when we once more
enjoy
to rest around the fire, and dream another dream.

*   *   *

Peace is a Melting Iceberg

What is the enduring longing in the soul of Mankind?
You tell me this is Peace …
How can it be otherwise?
For the soul of Mankind must be peaceful –
Who doubts this, doubts the truth of life.

*   *   *

The great White Bear rests above our heads,
pointing his toes towards the infinite Pole
about which the Universe rotates …
Hold onto this, and let the whirligig of Life
just carry on running around you.

*   *   *

Send a message to the Bear :-
"I'll hug you if you can come in and join me,
in this your glorious Constellation,
and by so doing, we can show the world
that Peace lies in your Soul, dear wise Bear,
as it does in mine, surely as it does in mine.

*   *   *

Let me hold your paw,
and lead me on a dance across the stars …
A breathless, airless transformation;
then the whole world can see us, waltzing from Venus to Mars,
tracking the spatial geometry of our intimate Planetarium.

*   *   *

The Great Bear says:-
"Don't hold onto me, for I'm a melting iceberg,
grasp instead the precious life within you,
hold it closely in your hands,
or it may melt away, leaving you with a mirage of reality.

*   *   *

***Tibetan Monastery by Lake in Himalayas.** What incredible effort and willpower was needed to build such fine Monasteries perched on sides of seemingly inaccessible cliffs! This Tibetan architecture expresses the power of beauty and truth enacted in the simple life of Tibetan Monks and Lamas. As mentioned in my other book, Poems for Cosmic Lovers, I enjoyed staying in a variety of Tibetan Monasteries while painting and wandering in the Indian Himalayas. Although this my painting is the result of many experiences there, it does depict how inspiring this life can be.*

Hear me, hear me cries our Earth!
My voices are many, do you not hear the distant calls
of many animals and birds as they die for the lack of
forage,
of insects too, their familiar drones and calls grow
fainter.

*   *   *

What must you do to stem the tide of powerful
machines
that multiply with devastating ease,
all having a special tonic breath,
like fierce black dragons breathing fire,
whose energies are drawn from deeply settled
mantles,
will their appetites ever be restrained?

*   *   *

You people, ask yourselves – what can I do to stem the
tide,
to let the good earth breathe well again?
to save the dying species and restore a reasonable
climate.
One needs to ask oneself, especially ones deeper self
"What must I do, what can I do?
Surely there must be something, however, small, that
I can do?"

*   *   *

Once, poorer Nations less mechanised,
have in twenty years become the most advanced in
wealth;
And now have raced ahead to build their overcrowded
cities,

where millions catch their breath in masks,
their Corporate master need to feed their greed,
while they grow fatter, if disillusioned,
they amply demonstrate the myth that happiness
means wealth.

*   *   *

It seems the human mind has certain flaws,
the greatest you may argue is this insatiable desire for
more …
The good Earth looks on in curios lament, saying: -
"Beware the mind whose cravings must eventually
destroy you,
not me, whose beautiful face may change, but not my
Life!
For my food is ultimately Cosmic"
You may wish to save me, but first you need to save
yourselves!

*   *   *

(Broadcast by Jeffrey on Sound Art Radio 102.5 FM
and online 26th June 2017)

"Storm, Rain and Light; the power of Human Unity"

High on tilted moons the soaring Northern gales,
are cutting vast grey clouds on the sharp tors.
Spinning millions of seeking souls descend in fiercely
billowing sheets.
Each holding a dream fulfilment, power and unity,
longing for the good green land's embrace, her gentle
hands;
as we land our gurgling cries are drowned by
deepening roars of thunder.

* * *

Now gathering into rills, we spill our sensual bodies
into kindred streams falling into green coombes,
where are plaintif songs begin to echo from crouching
rock walls
and massive boulders, making ever changing
symphonies.

* * *

In legions snaking ever downwards,
we carry our fearless energies to swing and curl from
step to fall,
now stars, now iridescent greens,
and now in all our fury we crash against these dark
immortal rocks,
so become infused with sparkling light,
to catch a glimpse of who we were, and who we
really are.

* * *

Knowing our latent power beyond all else upon this
Planet,
when once united we can shape whole mountain
gorges,
hurl trees and rocks into the air,
cave boulders into fluid forms more like themselves,
capitulating time and substance to our Royal will.

* * *

Sweeping all before, many streams make the Dart,
where at last we greet our powerful Mother,
longed for Goddess of this mighty confluence.
So now we cry, "We are the Goddess, we are
this ……. River,"
curving, swirling, racing seawards,
then we meet the final weir to rush headlong into
exploding foaming waves,
momentarily curling back into a ritualistic vortex
waltzing spin,
our transcendent marriage with the redemptive salt-
sea estuary is consummated!

* * *

Footnote: Early February 2004 is characterised by some wild
storms here over Dartmoor, and the white waters of the weir
outside my flat are explosions of the Goddess in triumphant
power

"SNOW GOOSE – One Belonging to the Horizon"

Over the great Lake Bolsena, amidst the Appenino,
the Lake of icy tears and joy,
you fly into the Western setting sun,
your head outstretched to greet the fire,
melting the sorrowful ice,
an ambassador of transcendence between Earth and Heaven,
your powerful streamlined wings and will
have freed the water in a flurry of spray,
beating the trembling airs into a submissive release!

*   *   *

I see you thus, cutting into the sun,
yet somehow embracing it, like some baby,
and my soul travels with you,
quite unable to resist such a vision of transcendent ecstasy.

*   *   *

This beauty, this vision of adventurous courage,
is the only language my soul can recognise.
A language so powerful, it draws my lonely soul
out of its body to join you,
to see through your eyes the receding Lake
edged by greens, then deep rock-indigos,
feeling great wings pressing the swiftly flowing airs,
hearing its whistling songs!

*   *   *

Here for once I've left the cloying tasks of earth life,
a soul not ultimately too constrained,
or too concerned by the daily needs of a body.
Dear heart, dear love, I'll ride with you,
through the receding clouds, soaring up into deepest indigo blue of the steady heavens.

*   *   *

Moving Swans

Swans at one with the rhythm of this River
and at one with the rhythm of life.
Who gave this swan his grace, his power his glory?
Can I but find some answers by entering his mind this
while,
so bless'd to have his mate, his wife for life . . .
Perhaps their secret lies in wordless resonance,
for words bring ideologies, religions and conflict.

*   *   *

A reddening Western sky bathes all in a redeeming
warmth;
the time is iright they feel to make ascent to fly
upstream . . .
Feeling the strength of giant wings, the swan presses
the air,
his head an outstretched envoy to the body's pulsing
rhythm,
with trailing webs the last to part the shining water
in a fury of spray, he's airborn!

*   *   *

His mate soon follows in streamlined grace,
they follow the familiar green reflective tunnel,
to find their roost, and watching all the while for
rising fish in fine awareness,
the oaks rush by like flickering movies,
their ethereal alto calls match the creaking steady
beating wings,
some local gardeners pause to listen . . .
and they're taken back to medieval castles,
where swans were kept to guard their Royal heritage.

*   *   *

Now they reach a widening pool
to make a quiet gliding slow descent,
their feet push forward to meet the water,
like hydrofoils in a flashing spume . . .
Now their bodies brush the surface, and familiar
buoyancy restored.

*   *   *

This is parable to explain
how when our body finds its frail demise,
one can decide to fly up to another fast vibration
if not quite ready to remain in this suspended
animation,
can fold ones wings to fall into another life,
another kind of being, and start once more
a fresh adventure in this richly beautiful Planet Earth.

*   *   *

On Waking In Kashmir

The scenes of my dreams emerge into this misty grey
light,
Prompted by the calls from many minarets meeting
Over this quite, sleeping lake in a heavenly symphony
My soul responds in ecstasy to be alive in this so
special place,
And amphitheatre of high mountains catching first
golden light,
Majestical above the mist.

*   *   *

This my mind sees as the grand conch-shell blown by
many men,
Somehow uniting them with this ancient Earth,
Himalayan backcloth of their lives,
These echoing voices blend to form a complex fugue,
A grand prayer of praise offered to the lords of all
creation,
An accidental fusion of polyphony, weaving a banner
of gold
Under this rising sun, whose birth has lately chased
away the stars.

*   *   *

As I turn on my side to gaze across this lightening
lake,
The shimmering gleaming Mosque hangs above the
mist footless,
Greeting this new born day like a reassuring father,
Ready to guide my light through this portal of
Heaven,
after gently sailing in this decorated ship across these
sacred waters,

Opening a vista of transcendence and ecstatic
enlightenment,
The awe inspiring beauty of all, here moves my soul
Into resonance with this Universe, and my mind!

*   *   *

Soon the other complicated sounds of life will join the
chorus –
Birdsongs, the solo flutes and voices, then later
motors with their horns,
Blend with the cocks calling proud to greet this vastly
rising sun.
All is a complex cadence falling into this limpid,
Wise reflective lake.

*   *   *

Footnote: This poem I dedicated to dear friend and patron,
Dr. Karan Singh who invited me to stay in his Palace in
Kashmir to do whatever landscape paintings I wished, and
gave me full hospitality of a guest wing of Karan-Mahal.
A most wonderful experience, and a whole sitting room of
the Palace is devoted to my paintings. He's remained a good
friend since then (1984), and I always visit him when in New
Delhi, where he has another smaller palace. He was Governor
of Kashmir for 30 years and much loved and respected by
all in India.

————•••————

26

Pilgrims climb to a Tibetan Monastery in High Himalayas: *This painting shows a combination of my experiences while staying in this fantastic region, mostly in Tibetan Monasteries, all the while painting. While this is a conjectural composition, it does depict the kind of dramatic scenery one enjoys here. For me this was the culmination of my long journey from Devon, England to the Indian Himalayas; but never in my dreams did I imagine that I would actually stay for periods as resident artist in some of the high Tibetan Monasteries. The Lamas made me very welcome to take part in their daily ceremonies, enjoying the sacred chants. My physical and spiritual health was always improving with this singing in the pure air!*

A Life, A River

Part I (A symphonic poem in 2 parts)

Conceived in love and fire.
The seeds lie deep in dark, tight, fissures,
While the women's pulse and warmth
Nurtures early stirrings of consciousness.

*   *   *

First this then will, desire, an appetite for minerals,
The tiny being becomes a babe,
While time and pressure builds a pool,
Rising towards the warmth and generosity of light.

*   *   *

As he ascends, the rocks less hard evolve to shale,
Then warmer earth, now resting time, and time ………
In waxing moon he stirs, then thrusts
With surging joy to feel free air.

*   *   *

This first russet resonance
Explodes into a glittering spray of diamonds,
Spinning the embracing air into a gorgeous flight of
colours,
Soaring rainbow aura to plunge to shattering glistening
stones,
Spiralling down to form a pool of min, will, identity.

*   *   *

Too soon this great adventure calling life,
Thrusts him out to join its shelter skelter, Ziggy zaggy
ways,
Where many a fall and rock will block yet momentarily
sway
His whirling, wild descent past emerald ferns,
Whose fleeting kisses feed a naked heart called beauty.

*   *   *

From this torrent swells a stream moulded by these
towering rocks
And shading trees, deeply diving into crystal pools,
To fill my nightly dreams with owls and tigers,
Preluding cascades roaring dawn.

*   *   *

Stretch my body, stretch my brain,
What's this mind that knows it's name?
Wind, swirl and curl anew,
These eyes can rarely fix a view.

*   *   *

Got my legs and got my frame,
Totter, run, laugh and leap,
Caress the pebbles with my feet,
Bubbling, sliding, slithering, crawling,
Rolling, falling, stumbling, bawling!

*   *   *

All the while my mother holds me,
Sees me, knows me, feeds me, scolds me.
Screaming, crying, demanding, calling,
Tears and shocks, it's so appalling!

*   *   *

Now I feel the need to see, expand and grow,
Yet rocks keep blocking, cutting my flow.
I'm smashed, deflected, guided, moulded,
Cajoled, conditioned, minced and scolded,
My spirit bruised, battered yet I know . . .

*   *   *

Where's the soul I so much long for,
Where's the heart I called my own,
Where's the guidance of my spirit,
Where's the love this mind has known?

*   *   *

Part II

Father, father tell me clear,
Whence I must be bound,
Will I reach the river soon,
Or will I run aground?

*   *   *

I see and feel the world around,
I know it's beauty deep within,
Yet this school you say I need,
Holds for me just boredom, tears and din.

*   *   *

As I plunge towards the River,

Curling, swirling, furling, widening;
In my dreams I'm deeply praying,
Angel hold me closely through these fires
Of passions, tensions, aches, desires.

*   *   *

Feed the brain ! dear Mama says,
Feed your mind and you'll survive.
Don't be swayed by your emotions,
Though your heart is full of pinings,
Fill it up with facts and findings!

*   *   *

So enswathed in such dilemmas,
Body cast midstream flow,
Will I drown in abstract factions,
Wearing clothes I hardly know,
Flinging books into a corner, when I reach my fireside
glow.

*   *   *

Here is freedom, love and care,
To climb the trees of soul desires,
Meeting myself in the forest,
Hunting the man with dog and longbow.

*   *   *

With my friends I walked the pines,
Swinging from top to top fearlessly
I am Adam and Hunter under the starlit heavens,
Proudly loosing arrows towards the starlit heavens,
Proudly loosing arrows towards the distant Orion,
Knowing my heart can forge them into gold
Flung back in meteoric sprays to feed the beauty,
And the deeps of this, my growing soulfulness.

*   *   *

"Journey to Paddington"

(On The Great Western Railway from Totnes, Devon
to London)

My train flies over the sea,
Deep blue streams into turquoise,
The hem of her dress streaked with golden white
As I enter the terracotta rock cliff,
The roar fills my eyes with darkness
Flecked with bright stars . . .
Yet soon the sea strand again and again,
Like snaps of childhood holidays,
Before another blackness in a quick dream.

*   *   *

Too soon the wide horizon closes,
In the gulls and stately wading geese,
Expanding again to the mud-flanked levels
With a parade of yachts before the farther hills and the
town,
While my eyes are thirsty for the old haunts
I so much loved in student days;
Each a story of some passion,
First bright, reflective, then depressed.

*   *   *

This train, my life, thrusts me ever forward
To adventures still to pass
In a shrinking world, Siberia seems a hair's breath
away,
And the golden moon is on our doorstep.
How fortunate to be born into an age of turmoil,
Caught in a whirlpool of ascending consciousness.
My role seems clear, to let it guide me where it will,
Unfathomable, this mystery called Life unfolds,
For me so full of fascination.

*   *   *

How much I love this train of life,
Surfing the green and golden fields
And sometime pools kissed by the vagrant sky.
Then the canal remembering slower ways of passage,
Fast past the drear grey factories,
Endless estates of boxy suburban housing,
Flashing stations, till, in time.
The gentle pull-back breaking into Paddington,
One great cathedral of nineteenth century enterprise,
Brunel saying: - "Here I am, this is my dream
expressed,
one grand focus for my web of rails canals and ships,
bringing cool steel, iron and clay,
from the fiery cauldrons of the North and West.

Conversation with a Sea Otter

Walking West from Craigdow Castle of the Muses,
the lane rises and dips by the Loch Goil,
sometimes screened by Birch and Rowan,
today grey clouds reflected in her face
seem just as ruffled silver fur.

*   *   *

This narrow camelback – like lane,
just like the ups and downs of life
is subtly guided by the steady,
shining levels of the loch close by.

*   *   *

Where the lane ends I turn to face the loch
to gaze across in wonder,
somehow expecting an event,
eitherin the air or under?

*   *   *

And then to spot the darkend head
so way beyond the rippling shore,
I try to focus consciousness
in joining with this unknown beast
my peaceful greeting.

*   *   *

The minutes pass, whcn suddenly
a whiskered head with eyes
stares up to fix me in a gaze but yards off shore, I
wave my arms then start a kind of dance
to semaphore my welcome.

*   *   *

Too soon he dives . . .
But I continue my connection
still hoping for his reappearance . . .
and yes, some minutes on
he comes inshore again
so with my opened brolly dance
we can prolong our conversation . . .

*   *   *

Who can now doubt this Otter
holds a mindful curiosity
and consciousness like mine . . .
but unlike me, is quite contented
with his sea-deep space
and briney air sublime.

*   *   *

I wrote this poem shortly after returning from my walk while staying in Carrick Castle of the Muses, Craigdow, overlooking Loch Goil, Scotland in September 2012, adding last verse in December 2012.

The Great Mystery of Love

Do we wish to know the mystery of love?
There are so many ways to love, and here I try to find a few
like life itself, so steeped in unified diversity,
all breathe the Cosmic air.
While listening to a great and splendid symphony,
I'm taken by a greater power than kisses with a passionate
lover.

*   *   *

Although so very different, there is a common thread,
and that's a rare ecstatic resonance they both enjoy.
This stimulating response to beauty
is just like diving in a crystal pool, to rise beneath the stars.

*   *   *

You may ask exactly how or why do we respond to beauty?
Can you recall how we are spiritual beings, just fluxed
together
when that primal seed was planted in a bed of love,
and then this magic wand of life swept by to make the
embryonic babe.

*   *   *

So now may I invite the babes to climb aboard this basket,
letting tethers fall away to rise above the earth,
so they can then behold the land below in all its glories,
while we do sing our lullabies to celebrate their freedom.

*   *   *

Can we now accept that Beauty is the catalyst
that gels the heart and mind into a state we aptly must call
love.
How bless'd we are to see and feel this ground of green and
gold,
found within the spectrum of our days . . .
From this, one can reflect that Love and Beauty merge
to make this life of ours so precious.

*   *   *

True love can happen when two Beings come together
to share their feelings, joys, ideas and creations,
while resonating songs of Natural Law;
and sexual pull must only be the spiritual gift,
but not the whole of love.

*   *   *

So what is Natural Law you ask?
One part is sure, there is a Law of Balance in this cyclic
universe,
wherein all giving is rewarded in some mysterious way,
so gifts must never be returned to giver.

*   *   *

Consciousness or Gods spirit upholds the substance of our
bodies,
as this pervades all space in this our starry Universe,
wherein all Beings can send their thoughts and love
to other beings or plants or trees beyond.

*   *   *

The mysteries of love are endless . . .
all are valid, all are true,
so here I've set out just a few,
that might just catalyse your views too?

*   *   *

One last word – when in darkness or in doubt,
just listen to the wisdom of your soul,
for therein lies clarity and the light to guide you there,
to where all problems fall away like raindrops on a
summers day.

*   *   *

Fire & Water

These days there's fire in my heart
and water in my soul.
By some subliminal accord they don't conflict.
Instead they seem to complement each other
in a kind of corporeal soft diplomacy.

*　　*　　*

This water has the blessed quality of eating fire,
so when it feels the battle flames arising,
looks on with quiet assurance,
like the sage under a Peeple Tree,
saying, you think you're free,
but in reality you'll self destruct when I come by
to eat you up, you'll see!

*　　*　　*

Of all the elements of this good Earth,
water is the peace maker,
the eternal giver of all life.

*　　*　　*

It just takes the passion of my heart and turns it into love.
& with encouragement, can send it round the world
the ultimate balm where fiery battles rage,
dear water always tries to quench the flames.

*　　*　　*

Meanwhile, I do reflect there is the passionate fire
in men's hearts and minds that must eventually learn
from soul that flames are only good,
when gathered into inspirational love.

*　　*　　*

The fire that makes the home a home,
can also make a battle ground for some,
tho' far away, their cries can come,
like desperate messengers across the crowded airways.
Always in readiness, the Water Goddess stands on
guard since this old world began.

*　　*　　*

Remembering Solstice, Turning of the Year

This is the turning of the year,
when we can halt a while to hear
the ever present quiet voice within,
whose gentle guidance never fails.

*   *   *

If only we can halt a while
our all too chattering minds,
and dive deep into the healing spring,
the very source of who we really are.

*   *   *

This source may seem as purely spiritual,
and yet we may reflect and see
the fabric of our beings is largely water,
so here's another source we're welded to,
this magic liquid giving life
to all on this fair Earth is ever binding.

*   *   *

This is the turning of the year,
when we can stop our clocks
to let our soulful selves emerge,
like incandescent flowers of Morning Glory.

*   *   *

When people of this world remember who they really are,
their inner conflicts will dissolve,
and then it will seem wrong
to fight another human being,
for we are all one family of souls, united by one God.

*   *   *

Journey of a Bar Headed Goose over Himalayas

How does it know, this Goose,
where to go?
Come first frost flakes of ice
in the great Northern Lake,
it's hard to fish, and little creatures burrow deeper.

*   *   *

So one day soon this leader Goose
decides its time to voyage South to warmer climes,
and sends around the signal to his skein in consciousness,
the news of imminent ascent,
"To the South" they call "to the warmer South".

*   *   *

This Goose stretches his wings, pressing the air,
thrusting head forward body following
his webbed feet skim the lake in spray,
while others swiftly rise, making a swishing turmoil.
Airborn, they call their familiar "Yes we can!"

*   *   *

Heading for the Great Himalayan Range,
they quickly reach the first pass,
Following the River, always getting higher,
soon the icy mountains start to close around,
and the air gets thinner.

*   *   *

These very special Geese fear not great attitude,
and have the inboard gear,
for needing little oxygen to keep ascending,
high over ice-bound peaks,
transcending usual limitations, they're easy
conquerors!

*   *   *

This Bar-Headed Goose has made
this annual migration for millennia
and built this into its whole mind, body and
consciousness,
we may marvel in wonderment,
yet these beautiful birds are simply born to be heroes!

*   *   *

During this flight the high level jet streams
are specially strong, tho 'not uniquely so,
our leader Goose knows how to weave minds,
how to adapt to every situation . . .
It's happened all before in his so ancient mind.

*   *   *

Battling with the winds, how does it feel,
for this wise pilot, this great pacemaker?
Perhaps some sense of triumph,
looking down upon the highest glacial ravines,
of these the greatest mountains of this world.

*   *   *

At last he spies, down beyond a break in clouds
some greenery, and so begins his long more restful
glides,

yet sometimes blown upwards a while
by the powerful thermal chimneys, then,
still pressing through, his slow descent continues . . .

* * *

Now below the clouds the first stream,
soon banked by trees, following its windings,
he knows they must so quickly find first stop,
for water and perhaps a tiny fish or snail,
before ascending yet again to feel the welcome warmth.

* * *

The stream becomes a River in the broader forest valley . . .
He has a picture in his mind, a favourite lake,
Where they may all pitch down in splendid formation,
to enjoy first feed after days of fasting,
under the warmth of this benevolent sky.

* * *

Embracing the Tor and Jerusalem

People of Britain, here we all are,
remembering Jerusalem . . .
Now as ever fulcrum of this world
where East meets West . . .
Palestinians confront Israelis.
May there be balance, may there be justice!

*   *   *

Many ancient links has Glastonbury with Jerusalem,
remembering those pioneers of peace,
Joseph and Jesus, ambassadors of non-violence,
speaking those eternal truths:
love all others, nurture the blessed Earth,
seeing the futility of violence!

*   *   *

People of Britain, here we all are
embracing this Tor,
while at this time, lovers of peace
are also encircling Jerusalem,
hoping for peace, longing for justice,
now we remember Jerusalem,
Salaam, Salaam, Salaam . . .
Ah-hum, Arhum; Aum Shanti, Aum Shanti, Shanti . . .

*   *   *

A Birthday Wish

My life is a great joy, brimming over with the pleasure to create in many fields within my gift of spirit,
these arts of painting, sculpture, architecture, poetry and music.
How generous my angels of inspiration!
Do these arts capture the fire and spirit of my being.

*   *   *

Yet still there is this longing, this yearning
for a closely intimate showing of these creative joys
with one woman who has this passion too.
Who rides the high surf of this worlds life,
whose eyes and poise can never hide
their overwhelming love of life.

*   *   *

Life, life, life!
Take us in your arms and feel the pulse of our being.
Draw out our gifts across this world,
let them shine in the great temples of our dreams,
and the Palaces of our desires.

*   *   *

For now is the turning of this teeming planet
to face an overwhelming light,
shimmering across the vastness of this Universe.
Who dare ride this ship of shocking fortune?
Whose is the mind who knows no bounds?
Whose soul can bear the flame of everlasting life?

*   *   *

Passport to Love

You are my singular passport to love,
this stamp on paper from above,
may lend some credence to my passion,
that surely in this while may come
to pass between us in a sudden run,
of mutually heated pleasure.

*   *   *

You have the light within your eyes,
to pull my heart and minds surprise,
across the border to an unfamiliar land,
where I, this single man, has no command . . .
And so, I beg you, take me by my hand,
to climb this barrier into bliss-filled light.

*   *   *

This land holds secrets yet untold,
of glittering castles lined in gold,
where we, the joyful pair may wander
freely past the lovely lakes into a magic woodland,
and there enfold each other in our fond embrace.
To find another place, even our dreams had seldom seen

*   *   *

Dance of Swifts

This great pleasure I have now in my new abode
to gaze out the large wide windows south,
watching the swifts and swallows,
as they soar, circle, dive, fall and swivel at great speeds.

*   *   *

Their dance reminds me of the restless thoughts of mind,
this wild monkey who fears most a peaceful silence
of dread inaction, or even a single aim like meditation,
this wondrous achievement of human evolution has this one defect.

*   *   *

As I gazed on, three wild geese flew high above the swifts
in a steady single-minded path.
How reassuring I thought,
For they're just like the ultimate steady guide of my soul.

*   *   *

My mind loves the beautiful unpredictable dance of swifts,
how it craves excitement and constant change . . .
Here lies the failing of this frantic world,
millions of minds tossed in a relentless sea
of every kind of media stimulation.

*   *   *

Dear Lord of my dreams I pray,
may I hear more the guidance of my soul,
enter calm waters, navigate my ship
towards the lovely harbour ruled by imaginative peace.

*   *   *

Our Souls are Non-Violent and Peaceful   24th February 2016

My friends the Jains, Buddhists and Hindus,
do hold the human soul is real and peaceful,
so greeting persons of any colour, race or calling,
with folded hands in Namastay is just the
peaceful way.

*   *   *

But the mind like some vast curiosity shop,
collects ideas, experiences, religions, desires, loves,
philosophies,
and even lovers in a greatly mixed up clutter,
its fine as long as some degree of openness is kept,
a window to another world, a new idea or beautiful
conception.

*   *   *

Ah, Buddhists speak of Mindfulness,
yet paradoxically their goal is mindlessness!
The greatest asset of this Path must surely be
compassion,
to build a loving awareness of the living beings
around us.
Doing Mahayana Ordination with the Dalai Lama was
for me
the start of strict non-violent regulation . . .
But ultimately is this really possible?

*   *   *

The Jains believe it is, tho' even they do drink their
milk,
flayal their rice and bake their breads,
we human beings do need the foods to feed our
energies,
just like all this dynamic living world.

*   *   *

How then to enact a peaceful life?
Today our minds too soon are deluged in the dross of
distractions,
media, noise, machines in this overcrowded world.
Fortunate I feel I've been to have the peace of
mountains,
Himalayas, Pyrenees and quiet peaceful gardens here
at home.

*   *   *

It's sad the human mind must have its constant
desires,
as it to keeps on saying "Here I am to serve you,
but don't neglect me or I'll die!"

*   *   *

Meditation, chanting to peaceful music
can offer respite to the restless mind.
For millennia, people of this world still love to chant
and sing.
The peaceful mind can dip into,
the treasure house of sub-conscious imagination.

On Wicklow Hills in Spring

Five hills crown the ancient landscape lined in golden
gorse,
and many shades of green.
Here a relic of some forgotten monastery stands
stranded
in the gently undulating waves,
I can feel the shining streams connecting time past
with time future.

*   *   *

For me here there is no time, only an overwhelming
presence,
a deluge of newness all emptying out of the sky –
it's good to feel warm inside this chariot,
as she fearlessly plurges through fiercely falling
waters,
these grey-green hills are rippling now,
as though caught in some complex musical rhythm
whose beat has suddenly quickened to reveal their
evolutionary history,
in a nano-second.

*   *   *

So now I view this ancient landscape,
not as the early man might have,
but through the safely toughened glass of modernerty.
While he cursed the wildly freezing rain lashing his
eyes,
as he traipsed his weary way,
longing for the bright fire in his earthen home,
and smiling wife's embrace.

*   *   *

So I see these lands, my mind washed clean
by the Spring cold rains;
and the lovely woman set before me warmly sensual,
smiles . . . springing a lever in my heart,
setting another storm in motion.
Out there I am with him, only my rain is tears of
passion,
to be quenched only by her soft enfolding.

*   *   *

Who Am I

No need to ask me who I am,
only God knows, so ask God;
and there will be the answer:
just listen to the wind on a wild night,
or the waves breaking on a stoney strand,
hear the storm surfing the sparkling beaches!

*   *   *

Our honest God will say,
this man is that, all that, and so am I,
His dear soul is such a distillation of all that,
he sings with my voice,
he speaks with my words,
he paints in my amazing colours!

*   *   *

This man is born within my love,
so if he's true to his soul's mission,
he'll radiate this love to all he meets,
to all life's myriad manifestations;
from tallest trees to tiniest insects,
riding life's waves he must surely know this love?

*   *   *

And who is God again you say?
Will this man answer if he's true,
that God is life, and life is everywhere,
a part of me and a part of you,
so when you speak with God,
you're only speaking with your deepest self,
and all of life, as that too is part of you.

*   *   *

Falling down from greenery hills,
this Town is gathering round the ancient Castle,
so proud to be diverse and mixed in architecture,
while in its self-enriching creativity, can cast
in many fields beyond its porous walls,
to float on down the Dart to join the open seas,
of ideas, philosophies or modes of being,
beyond the usual normal English way.

*   *   *

Here its people don't just sow creative seeds,
but help to build the ground for sharing them
within enriching gardens, and their music, poems,
paintings, skills, tools, energies, foods and healings.

*   *   *

Beneath this canopy of transcendental transformation,
some people know its safe to walk outside
the usual fears confirming their imagination,
to let their minds go free to fly beyond material needs,
and join the greater realms of consciousness.

*   *   *

Totnes Town transitionally transcending,
how do you read your residents now,
when your legacy records one thousand years?
Do they pioneer new values durably,
and roots to happiness in sharing what they have?

*   *   *

Why should life all labour be,
lets get together and see
how we can build a life,
where common wealth becomes normality.

*   *   *

A Song of Christmas

Not so softly this shining town prepares itself,
for the annual rising tide of stressed-out shoppers,
who glide and jostle along its streets . . .
Frantic sleepwalkers seeking something seemingly special,
in this December parade of dumbed-down banalities.

*   *   *

Let's have a Carnival, let's have a Ball;
let us pretend we've imagined it all!
Tear down the pretence of Christian fervour;
we'll remember our roots and baptise at the Well,
and process down the streets to the sacred old River,
singing our chants with torches held high;
here's to our Goddess for to all she's the giver!

*   *   *

Down there breathing deeply the sea-river air,
we'll light the great fire to share bread and wine,
call out the Goddess with our cymbols and chimes,
while launching so tenderly our floating ships,
gazing at flames born along in the cups of her hands,
some race ahead and some fall behind.
Thus are our souls bound up in currents of fortune?
Or can we take charge by the will of the mind?

*   *   *

London in 1999 – Towards the Millenium

Where is the optimistic vision for the millennium?
Only I hear a catalogue of fears,
visions vamping up the dear dross of a thousand years.
O man, where are your forsight dreams ringed in shining gold?

* * *

You watch the River flowing by your timepiece,
fearfully restoring forts to shield and shroud your past glories,
while building monuments to fun and vapid pleasures.
You're good at casting currencies in a blind date with a cosy future,
while Southern millions sweat and sell themselves
in the dust of a forgotten world,
only for you to build tall towers, from which to gaze down
at the squalid dull grey blocks desperately trying to remember
their identity, beyond these mere pounds in square footage.

* * *

Where is this prostitute called time,
is she hidden in these chip fed screens?
Mysteriously reduced to cyphers helplessly, hopelessly,
nicely packed into capsules cast out into space.
Before the mechanistic clock she was the waltz of our Sister Moon,
and the seasoned round of our glorious Father Sun.

* * *

O Man, these calibrated beats
Can't drown these ancient periodic pulls of distant planets.
Our hearts's irregular rhythm, is what we long for,
remembering the love we have, can span the universe.

* * *

Time for Love

Time may come and time may go, but love goes on forever,
some there are who sometimes say, I haven't time for love.
Surprised they are when I do say 'that love has time for them'.
The Earth and all that therein lives.

*   *   *

The greatest pleasure is to wander in the woodlands
and the moor, or rest a while on wild sea strand,
feeling the wind is cleansing caress . . .
what better way to spend the day,
letting Nature breathe you, hold you, feed you.

***

If you feel too down, then don't despair . . .
Walk out the door holding your hand of intuition,
to guide you where you need to go . . .
Have trust this healing hand will take you
to the gardens, park, the lake or sea.

*   *   *

Very well you city dwellers say,
I haven't time to wonder out this day.
My job, my kids are first priority . . .
Perhaps when time allows I'll take your tip,
and make a trip to Nature land,
escape the claustrophobic city's hand.

*   *   *

Is this all there is I wonder sitting here?
Why cannot the country come to me?
There's always a super wildlife film to see,
here at home on my T.V.,
so why to suffer stress of wind and rain,
when all one needs to do is dream.

*   *   *

Time and Light

Time itself is an illusion –
it is only the reasonable rotations
of this planet Earth around the Sun,
and in turn the daily axial spin upon a mythical point.

*   *   *

Time future and time past
meet at zero point where time is lost,
and all times may be found,
if you can stop your mind?

*   *   *

For its one's mind that always longs for the next moment,
since without its perpetual passing,
the mind itself is lost,
and can only be redeemed by the soul.

*   *   *

If you or I can only say,
let soul control the way we pass the day,
each moment there must be,
all the vision we may need to see eternity.

*   *   *

For in Eternity may lie the key to happiness,
where time becomes irrelevant,
one moment is a lifetime,
so we may have so many lifetimes.

*   *   *

What blessing is the turning of this Earth,
that makes the night and makes the day,
for night is gateway for our dreams in timeless sleep.
Where minds set free to come to roam and play.

*   *   *

Trust and Sacrifice

In trust I dive from cliff into a sapphire pool,
while breathlessly I fall towards a gleaming sea,
the air carries me hawk like down, down,
till I smash the boyant skin, eyes tight shut in shock!
Then sounds of bubbling singings in my head, soothing;
and plunging deeper, holding fast my mouth.
I trust my lung full air will pull me upwards . . .
Then, gaining confidence opening eyes, I wonder
at the view of silver herrings seemingly oblivious,
while gently waving golden Bladrock forms a back drop
in this magic mariners landscape.

*   *   *

Slowly rising to the mirrored light
I'm thrust out dolphin-like into the sparkling waves,
this much more mobile other world of not yet real reality . . .
turning on my back to float and gaze into the indigo sky
I can reflect that here its Heaven, and there is Heaven too!

*   *   *

To live life fully brings a daily challenge,
so this dive and rise is mine today, to justly test my faith in life.
Surely such a small sacrifice with such a great reward.
I do believe that trust and sacrifice are closely intertwined,
my root to happiness must be to find the golden balance of the two.

*   *   *

The Spiritual Power of Nature

From trees, to rivers, to earth and mountains,
nature, the Cosmos has enormous powers we yet can barely comprehend,
the humble artist watches, waits, wonders, sees deeply,
and then with mindful love and light conceives some
beautiful work – a painting, building, garden, craft, invention.

*   *   *

The gifted one can translate some vast secrets of Life,
of this richly complex, beautiful planet, into art.
For I see myself as a diviner of energetic beauties
in the ever complex Cosmos.

*   *   *

For me the greatest finest works of art are born out of
this mystic act, beyond mere seeing,
but transcending & distilling the outer world through mindful
sensibility, into colours, movements, moods and rhythms,
to make a kind of visual music.

*   *   *

Art can emerge when the deeper spiritual self
is allowed to fuse with Nature of the outer world;
through our mystic gift of consciousness, we're all connected
with Nature inextricably – so all I need is to open the flow,
this stream of connectedness in meditation,
for the alchemical act of creation to appear.

*   *   *

I find the media of water-based colours very good,
to open this flow - the subtle fusions of colours, forms
and symbols can sometimes send the viewer into reverie!

*   *   *

N.B. This is not meant to be a poem, but a way to try to understand my way of letting Nature sing her songs in visuals ~ So all I can do, is share these thoughts with you.

To the Cosmic Fire Bride, St. Bridget

Lovely you,
hold me to your breast
and bid me enter the portal of your wisdom,
you are my guide into the spiritual Cosmos,
and my supreme self.
The memory of you will live forever in my soul,
quite beyond this mind stuff!

*　　*　　*

Lovely you,
when we hold each other very close,
our fusion sparks a signal to the stars…
here is love, may it beam across the Universe!
May it stoke the fires of consciousness,
enjoining the Sun's ancient passion for Mother Earth,
spawning children like the Moon.

*　　*　　*

Lovely you,
Drawing my flame inside you,
seeking my spark across this timeless void,
the door is opened to greet a wanderer,
and the shining Bridget touches me with her green Birch Rod,
Wrapping her cocoon around this passion,
giving her blessing and mystical support…
bchold, a new Being, a consciousness is born!

*　　*　　*

Tsunami

One fair day, on sun-soaked Eastern shores,
gold on indigo blue,
the birds, elephants & dogs fell silent,
wary of the innocent calm,
start running at the feeling while they can, inland.

*   *   *

The good Earth had felt it time
to vent her rage at the steady spoiling
of the delicate yet ancient balances of her
countenance,
by many a greedy industrialist,
mindlessly, mechanistically plundering her Ocean
gifts.

*   *   *

She breathed in deeply,
casting a fire-filled exhalation, under the sea so still,
first drawn back, the inhalation prefacing a fear,
as waters previously so calm are suddenly sent
soaring
skywards, by angry molten rocks,
pitching her face into a seething, foaming boiling
cauldron.

*   *   *

Forcing a purple breeze, soon felt on fearful faces,
this Ocean did her best to cushion Earth's rage,
only people living on the edge began to run,
or climb the sparsely scattered mangroves,
in vain attempts and desperate fear
to save themselves, their wives or children dear.

*   *   *

This friendly wall of death rolled on,
remorselessly engulfing all & everything before;
a beautifully demonic, seething swallowing giant,
her splendid glistening purple-green cloak,
spread in a sweeping scythe of vengeance!

*   *   *

Most days murmuring quietly to herself,
this Ocean is a friend, nurturer of men & fish,
not least the idle tourists who frolic in her waves!
Who then can blame her when, the greedy cityites
have cut the mangroves, fenced the strands, starved
the fisherfolk,
cracked her fine-tuned songs, if she unwittingly
rebels,
who can blame her?

*   *   *

Ways to World Peace

There are many ways to World Peace;
surely it starts with the human mind,
a mind so clever at solving problems,
and at inventing new machines,
new bombs, rockets, pesticides and mobile phones!

*   *   *

Life gets faster every day,
so fast we lose sight of our true selves,
deluges of facts bounce around our minds,
like ice hail in a wild storm!

*   *   *

And yet we do still long for peace,
a voice that still cries out beneath the synaptic noise,
"Slow down – listen please, this is the true story
of who you're really meant to be,
this tale of a peaceful soul hiding somewhere,
deep down there, that can sometimes emerge in dreams,
or in quiet meditation and reflection.

*   *   *

This must be the way of truth,
the way to personal peace in our time is possible…
World Peace will only come,
when all of us can quieten down to have some fun,
slow down enough to enjoy the Sun.

*   *   *

Your feedback please

Contact me on tel. 01803 866349 (pref); or *jeffrey@worldpeacegardensnet.org*

Printed in the United States
By Bookmasters